The Great Discovery

MANDY LOADER

Level 3

Series Editors: Andy Hopkins and Jocelyn Potter

Pearson Education Limited
Edinburgh Gate, Harlow,
Essex CM20 2JE, England
and Associated Companies throughout the world.

ISBN 0 582 42730 4

This edition first published 2000

NEW EDITION

Copyright © Penguin Books Ltd 2000
Illustrations by Bruce Hogarth
Cover design by Bender Richardson White

Typeset by Bender Richardson White
Set in 11/14pt Bembo
Printed and bound in Denmark by Norhaven A/S, Viborg

Published by Pearson Education Limited in association with
Penguin Books Ltd, both companies being subsidiaries of Pearson Plc

For a complete list of the titles available in the Penguin Readers series please write to your local
Pearson Education office or to: Marketing Department, Penguin Longman Publishing,
5 Bentinck Street, London W1M 5RN.

Contents

Introduction

Tim looked at the wonderful gold bracelet around the girl's wrist. He closed his eyes. Was it possible to discover one of the most exciting tombs of the ancient world? The tomb of Queen Cleopatra? The tomb of the beautiful Queen who chose to die by snake bite?

'If I can discover Cleopatra's tomb, I'll be famous!' he thought. 'It will be the biggest and most exciting discovery since Carter discovered the tomb of Tutankhamun!'

The girl looked out of the window. Her beautiful face looked sad.

Can Tim really discover Cleopatra's tomb? Who is the mysterious girl, and why is she wearing the ancient bracelet? Why does she look sad? Why does she want Tim to go back to England? Who is the Professor, and what does he want with Tim?

When Tim tries to answer these questions, he finds himself in trouble – big trouble. There is a curse on the tomb – the curse of the ancient white cobra that watches over the treasure inside it. Will Tim live, or will he die?

Mandy Loader spent several weeks in Egypt a few years ago. She visited the tombs of the ancient pharaohs and saw their beautiful jewellery in Cairo Museum. She had the idea for this story in the back streets of Alexandria!

Other readers by Mandy Loader are: *The Magic Ring, Can You Believe It?, The Lost Room, The Black Pearl, The Quest* and *The Woman of Iron*. Mandy Loader also wrote the new *Linguaphone English Language Course* (1995-96) and *Ozmo* (1998-99), a BBC course of English language videos for children. Before she began writing, she taught English in Paris, Tokyo and Rabat (Morocco). She now lives in England with her husband Shane and their three young children.

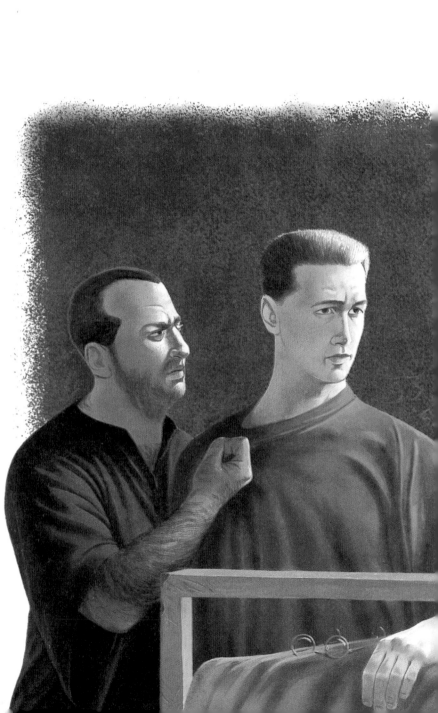

Chapter 1   In the Prison

Tim Saunders sat in the narrow room and looked at the floor. There was only one other man in the room with him.

'So you're going to leave us tomorrow?' the other man said.

Tim Saunders looked at him. He didn't smile.

'What are your plans? What will you do?'

Tim got up and walked away.

'Are you going back to England?' The man walked after him. 'You're not very friendly, are you?'

'I don't want to talk, Ahmed. Leave me alone.'

'You don't want to talk. That's nice! Shall I tell you something? You've been here for five years, and you've never wanted to talk. But I want to talk to *you*. I've wanted to talk to you since they put me here with you a week ago.

And I'm going to talk to you now, and you're going to talk to me.' He moved close to Tim.

Tim turned and pushed him away.

'Getting angry, are you? That's not very nice.' Ahmed put his face − a hard, ugly, criminal face − close to Tim's face. 'Now just stay calm, and we'll have a nice little talk,' he said. 'We've been together for a week, and you're leaving the prison tomorrow.'

Tim said, 'I've got nothing to say to you. Leave me alone.'

Ahmed smiled. He began to laugh − a hard laugh. 'Tell me about the girl. What was her name? Ah, yes, Maria.' He saw surprise on Tim's face, and he laughed. 'Maria, Maria, my pretty little Maria!' Ahmed sang.

He began to dance around the narrow room. Tim got up quickly and walked towards him.

'What do you know about Maria?'

'Oh, so you're speaking to me now, are you? You want a nice little talk now, do you?'

'What do you know about Maria? Tell me,' said Tim.

'I'll tell you what I know about Maria. And you tell me about the bracelet. OK?'

Tim sat down. His face was white.

'Most of Cairo knows about the bracelet,' Ahmed said. Then he continued. 'Or most of the people here know about it. But they don't know enough. They all want to know more. Will they leave you alone when you leave this place tomorrow? What do you think?'

There was the sound of a key in the lock. Both men turned and looked at the door. It opened, and a guard came in. He looked at Tim.

'Are you all right, Mr Saunders? You look pale. What's the matter?'

There was no answer. The guard looked at Ahmed. 'Are you making trouble?' he asked.

No answer.

'Maybe we'll give you your own room for your last night,' the guard said to Tim. 'We don't want anything to happen to you – not on your last night. Come with me. Only a few more hours, and then you'll be free.' The guard pulled Tim to his feet. 'Here, don't forget your glasses.' He picked them up and gave them to Tim.

'I'm sorry. I didn't feel very well for a minute. But I'm OK now.'

The guard helped Tim out, and unlocked another heavy door.

'Now, Mr Saunders, you can lie down in here.'

Tim lay on the hard bed. He could see the hot Egyptian sky through the small window. He took off his glasses, closed his eyes and listened to the sounds of the town. He could hear some men talking loudly in the narrow streets. He could hear some children laughing and playing near the prison. He could hear music on a radio. He could hear the shouting of people as they sold bread, fruit, sweets and vegetables. It was market day. And then he heard a woman singing. She had a lovely voice. She was very close, and he could hear the words of the song:

'I lost my love so long ago,' the woman sang sadly. 'Now there's only pain, there's only pain, pain and loneliness . . .'

Tim put his hands over his ears to shut out the song.

'Only one more day,' he said to himself. He looked at his hands. They were pale and thin. They looked like the hands of an old man. 'Maybe she's changed. Maybe she's forgotten me. Maybe she's got married. Maybe . . .' He stopped to listen to the end of the song.

'Maria,' he said softly. 'Maria.' He repeated the name again and again for the first time in five years. Those long, hot, lonely days were filled with thoughts of her, but he never spoke her name. He remembered again her face, her beautiful dark eyes, her laugh. He remembered the way that she moved. He lay in the narrow prison room and remembered their first meeting. It was more than five years ago, on a train from Cairo to Alexandria. He could picture it so clearly. The crowds and the noise of Cairo main station five years ago seemed to be all around him in his memory.

Chapter 2   The Bracelet

Cairo main station, on that day five years ago, was full of people. It seemed to Tim that they all wanted to get onto the Alexandria train. He reached the platform at last, and put down his suitcase. He searched through his pockets for his ticket, found it and got onto the train. He didn't notice the two people who were watching him closely.

The two people pushed their way to the ticket office, talked to the assistant, and hurried back through the crowds to the train.

Tim found his place and sat down. He took a book out of his pocket.

After a time, the train began to move. Tim took off his glasses and put down his book. He looked through the window. It was early morning and there were crowds of women in the streets. They talked in front of the piles of tomatoes and oranges that the country people brought to the city each day. Girls carried bread, and men carried heavy bags to the market. Tim watched happily. Business was as usual in Cairo.

The houses became fewer, and at last the train ran between the rich fields along the River Nile. For a time, Tim watched the country people at work. Then he sat back and looked at the passengers opposite him. They were a man and a girl. The man wore a pair of blue jeans and a black jacket. He was quite a handsome young man, but his eyes were hard. The girl was in European dress. She had expensive shoes on her feet and a lot of gold rings on her fingers. Tim looked at her face – at the smooth skin, the dark eyes, the narrow nose, the beautiful mouth, the long, straight black hair.

'Lovely,' Tim thought. 'She's as lovely as Queen Nefertiti. But she's not Egyptian. Where's she from?'

The girl looked out of the window. She didn't seem to notice Tim. The man spoke to her. She shook her head and continued to look out of the window.

The man spoke to her again. The beautiful girl slowly turned away from the window. Very slowly – Tim thought – she opened her bag. She took out a mirror. Then she lifted her hand to push back her hair. Tim's heart stopped. He shut his eyes, opened them and looked again. He searched through his pockets for his glasses, found them on the seat, put them on, looked again. It was impossible, but there it was, in front of his eyes.

Tim looked at it carefully for a long time. The bracelet was shaped like a snake – like a cobra, the snake of the Ancient Egyptian pharaohs. The cobra's body passed three times round the girl's wrist, and its head rested on the back of her hand. The eyes of the snake were red. They were two large, shining red jewels.

'Gold. Cobra shape. Unbelievable!' Tim thought. It was the most beautiful example of ancient jewellery. 'If it's real, it was made about 2,000 years ago,' he thought. 'How did that lovely girl get a bracelet like that?'

Tim looked carefully at the bracelet again. It wasn't like most Ancient Egyptian jewellery that he knew. Was it from the tomb of one of the pharaohs, the ancient kings? The type of work on the bracelet looked very late. That meant it was from a late tomb.

'But that's impossible!' Tim thought. 'Nobody has discovered any of the tombs of the last pharaohs yet.'

Tim Saunders was an archaeologist. Like other archaeologists, he knew that the tombs of the last pharaohs were in the north of Egypt, near Alexandria. But nobody knew exactly where these tombs were.

'I'd really like to find one of those undiscovered tombs,' Tim thought. He took off his glasses and looked out of the window.

'But which pharaoh?' he said to himself. 'Very late – 2,000 years old – late Ptolemy – the wonderful gold bracelet of a woman. A bracelet for a queen to wear. A bracelet that one of the most beautiful women in the world wore. A bracelet that perhaps belonged to the thirteenth and last of the Ptolemaic kings and queens. Cleopatra!' he said quietly. 'Is it from the tomb of Cleopatra, the most famous of the queens? Did that bracelet really belong to the great Cleopatra? Perhaps she was wearing it when she killed herself!'

Tim looked at the wonderful gold bracelet around the girl's wrist. He closed his eyes. Was it possible to discover one of the most exciting tombs of the ancient world? The tomb of Queen Cleopatra? The tomb of the beautiful Queen who chose to die by snake bite?

'If I can discover Cleopatra's tomb, I'll be famous!' he thought. 'It will be the biggest and most exciting discovery since Carter discovered the tomb of Tutankhamun!'

The girl looked out of the window. Her beautiful face looked sad.

Chapter 3   Tim Goes to Alexandria

The questions raced, one after the other, through Tim's mind:

'Is it really ancient? It doesn't look like modern jewellery. Is it real? If it's not, it's very well made. Did it belong to a pharaoh? If it did, it will have the pharaoh's name on it. The name will be on the inside of the bracelet, or on the side of the cobra's head. There will be a name! A bracelet like that is surely from a pharaoh's tomb!'

Tim looked at the girl. 'What am I going to say to her?' he

thought. 'Does she speak one of the languages that I know?'

'Excuse me,' he said. He tried to keep his voice quiet and calm as he spoke. The girl didn't answer. He tried again in Arabic. Tim's Arabic was good, but she still didn't seem to hear him. He put out his hand to touch her arm.

'Excuse me—'

The young man caught Tim's wrist. 'Do not touch her!' His voice was loud and angry. He spoke in English, but it wasn't the English of an Englishman.

The other passengers looked at them. Tim said, 'I just wanted to ask her something. She didn't answer when I spoke to her. I'm not going to hurt her.'

The young man continued to hold Tim's wrist. 'What do you want to know?' he said in a lower voice.

'I only wanted to ask her about the bracelet that she's wearing. I saw it a minute ago. It's a beautiful piece of jewellery. It looks very old.'

The man looked carefully at Tim. He didn't look friendly. 'OK, you can ask her. But I'll speak to her first.'

He spoke to the girl. Tim didn't understand what he said.

The girl looked at Tim. 'You like my bracelet?' She spoke very good English.

'Where's she from?' thought Tim. 'She isn't English and she isn't Egyptian.' Then he smiled at the girl and said, 'Yes, I like your bracelet very much. It's beautiful. Can I see it, please?'

The girl looked at the young man. He said something to her and she took off the bracelet and gave it to Tim.

The bracelet felt heavy in Tim's hand. He was sure it was real. He turned it over and searched for a name, the name of the pharaoh, the owner of the bracelet. He found the name on the cobra's head.

'KLE-U-PA-TRA – Cleopatra,' he said quietly.

'What?' said the young man.

'Nothing – nothing,' Tim said.

Was this the first step on the road to a great discovery?

'If I discover the tomb of the great Cleopatra,' he thought, 'I'll become famous around the world. And I'll be the first man in 2,000 years or more who has seen the most beautiful face in the ancient world.'

'It's very nice,' said Tim, as he gave the bracelet back to the girl. His hands shook a little. He hoped the girl and her brother didn't notice.

'Yes, it is,' replied the girl. 'My father says it's very old.'

'Where did you get it?'

'It was my mother's. She gave it to me before she died.'

There was a silence as the girl put the bracelet back on her wrist.

'My name's Tim Saunders. I'm an archaeologist. I work for London University.'

'My name is Felix. Her name is Maria. She is my sister.'

Maria. Tim liked the sound of the name. 'Maria, tell me, where did your mother get that bracelet?'

'It has been in our family for a very long time.'

Felix said, 'My father has other things like it at home.'

Tim didn't want to sound too interested. He asked quietly, 'What things?'

'Other bracelets, jewellery, rings – oh, quite a lot of things.'

'Can I come and see them? Will you show them to me? If they are real, they will be of great interest to my university. You can get a lot of money for them, too.'

'We don't need money.'

'Please can I come and see them?'

Felix was silent. He looked out of the window. The train ran along the side of a small river. There was plenty of activity in the river and on its banks.

'Can I come?'

'What are you doing here in Egypt?' asked Felix.

'I came here for a meeting of archaeologists in Cairo. The meeting ended yesterday. I decided to come to Alexandria to visit a museum or two. Then I'll enjoy the beach at Ramleh.'

'OK, you can come,' Felix said at last. He smiled. Tim didn't like his smile very much.

10

'Thank you. Thank you very much.'

Tim picked up his book, but his mind was busy with other things. The train stopped only at the important stations of Benha, Tanta and Damanhur. Tim usually enjoyed looking at the sellers of sweet cakes and cold drinks on the platforms. Passengers shouted their orders through the windows of the train, and the sellers passed up the cakes or drinks to them. But today was different. Tim watched with less than his usual interest.

He tried to read again. It was an interesting book about the position of women in the ancient world. But it failed to hold his interest. He was glad to see Lake Maryut with its fishing boats through the window.

Maria picked up her bag. 'Alexandria in five minutes,' she said.

'Do you live there?' Tim asked.

'Yes. Our home's in Alexandria.'

The train pulled slowly into the station. Felix pushed through the crowd. Tim and Maria followed him.

Chapter 4   The Treasure

'Where do you live?' Tim asked.

'In the old town,' said Felix.

'Yes, but where in the old town? What's your address?'

'The old town,' replied Felix. 'Just the old town!' He laughed. Tim didn't like his laugh, but he followed him. After a time, they left behind them the wide streets with their modern shops and the noise of cars, buses and lorries. They began to walk along narrower streets. The shops were smaller and more interesting. They sold brightly-coloured cloth for dresses, shoes and boots, cooking pots and every kind of food. And there were shops where people made things out in front, near the street. You could see them at work, making shoes, clothes, bread, cakes.

The streets were very crowded and Felix walked fast. He and his sister seemed to pass through the crowds without difficulty. Tim followed as quickly as he could with his suitcase. He knew some of the old town of Alexandria, but not this part. He looked behind him.

'Aren't we going round in circles?' he asked. 'I'm sure we went past that shop five minutes ago!'

Felix didn't reply, and Maria hurried on. He almost lost them in the crowd.

'Can you walk more slowly, Felix? I can't go so quickly with this suitcase. And where are we? Is it far?'

Felix said nothing. He kicked a cat that lay in the sun at the side of the street. The cat ran away.

'Hey!' shouted Tim. 'Poor cat! Don't do that!'

Tim was completely lost. All the streets looked the same. Each street had the same little shops, the same happy children, and the same unhappy-looking cats.

'Not far,' Felix replied. He kicked a thin and hungry dog that sat near a small café.

'Will you please stop kicking animals?' asked Tim.

Felix didn't answer.

At last they stopped in front of an old wooden door. There was no name or number on it. They knocked and waited. They heard a voice from behind the door, and Felix shouted something. The door was opened by an old woman, who took them inside.

Tim looked around in surprise. They were in a large, sunny garden. There were many beautiful flowers in the garden. The air was full of the smell of the small white flowers of the orange trees that grew there. In the centre of the garden there was a large pool. The doors in the walls round the garden were painted bright blue, and a little bird sang in one of the trees.

'What a lovely place!' Tim said.

Maria looked at him and smiled.

'Come and meet my father, the Professor,' she said.

An old man in white sat under the orange trees. He welcomed Tim and invited him to sit down. Tim looked round for Maria, but she was already behind one of the blue wooden doors.

'Before we talk, you must eat and drink,' Maria's father said. 'Aisha? Aisha! Bring some coffee!'

After a short time the old woman came into the room with coffee and a plate of cakes.

Tim wasn't hungry or thirsty, but he drank two cups of coffee and ate some cakes. At last he felt he could ask the question.

'I'm an archaeologist, Professor. Your daughter has an interesting bracelet. I think it's very old. Felix says you have other pieces like it. Will you show them to me, please?'

At first the old man didn't seem sure. Then he spoke a few words, and Felix got to his feet and went inside the house. He came out again a few minutes later with a large wooden box, and placed it on the floor in front of his father. The old man put his hand into a pocket and took out a key.

Tim watched with growing excitement. The old man put the key into the lock and turned it. His movements seemed terribly slow. Then he opened the box and, one by one, lifted out his treasures. He put them on the ground in front of Tim. First, a gold ring, with the same cobra shape as Maria's bracelet. Then other jewellery: a wonderful gold cup, and some other heavy gold rings. Then a beautiful head-dress. Tim looked carefully at the treasures, one after the other. They all had the same name on them: 'Cleopatra'. There were a number of gold belts and a pair of little golden shoes.

'She was very small,' Tim thought.

He looked at the wonderful perfume bottles and the beautiful pots for make-up.

'So this is how Cleopatra made herself beautiful for Mark Antony,' he thought.

He asked the old man, 'Where did you get all these things
from?'

'They have been in our family for a long time,' the old man
replied.

'But where did the treasure come from in the beginning?'

'Our family worked as treasurers to the pharaohs. That is what my father and grandfather told me. This treasure belonged to a pharaoh. After the pharaoh died, it was stolen. But from that time, the thief had terrible dreams. He couldn't sleep, and he couldn't eat. Soon after that, the thief died, too. The treasure was given back to the pharaoh's treasurer to look after. Ever since that time, the treasure has been in our family. That is the story.'

'Do you believe the story?'

'I don't know.'

'I don't know, either,' Tim thought. 'The Professor and his family are clearly not Egyptians. But we know that the Ptolemaic pharaohs employed Greeks and other foreigners. So the story is possible. And the Professor doesn't know that the pharaoh was probably Cleopatra!'

Chapter 5   A Mysterious Warning

'Can I photograph these things, please?'

'No. No photographs. I'm sorry.'

'But why not?' asked Tim.

'I don't want other people to know about the treasure.' The Professor got up. 'Please excuse me. I am an old man. I must rest.'

'But listen. If these things are very old, they should be in a museum. They should be in the Egyptian Museum in Cairo!'

'No. No photographs,' the old man repeated.

'I won't tell anyone where I saw these things. Can I take some photographs if I promise you that? Please.'

The old man didn't answer immediately. Suddenly they heard a shout: 'No!'

They looked round. Maria stood in a doorway.

'Don't do it, Mr Saunders!' she said. 'Don't take the photographs. You should go away!'

'Silence!' The Professor went to Maria. He looked angry. Then he turned and smiled at Tim. 'Yes, you can take photographs,' he said. 'But you must never say where you found them.'

'I promise,' said Tim.

The Professor and Felix got up and left. Maria cried quietly, her face in her hands. Tim went to her.

'Why don't you want me to stay?' he asked. 'I'll go when I've taken these photographs.'

Maria said nothing.

Tim picked up the first of the treasures, and put it against a wall. He took out his camera.

'Oh, no!'

Maria stopped crying. 'What's the matter?'

'I haven't got a film! I don't believe this! ' he said.

He looked round. Maria was watching him. There was a strange look in her eyes.

'Have you got a film or a camera that you can lend me?'

'I haven't got a film, but I've got a camera. Only a small one.'

'That doesn't matter.'

Tim waited until Maria brought him the camera. She smiled as she gave it to him.

'I hope it's all right,' she said. 'It's almost new.'

Tim put his hand out to take the camera. But suddenly it fell onto the hard floor.

Maria picked it up. 'It's broken,' she said.

'Your new camera! I'm terribly sorry! I must buy you another one.'

'You can't, not here. You can't buy cameras in the old town. But it doesn't matter. '

Tim looked at the broken camera.

Maria said, 'You must go now. You can't do anything here. Forget these things that you have seen.'

'Maria, what's the matter? Why are you saying this?'

There were tears in her eyes as she looked at Tim. 'I – I don't want–'

'Maria!' Her father's voice was hard. 'Go to your room. Stay there. Have you taken your photographs, Mr Saunders?'

'No. I haven't taken any photos – I haven't got a camera with a film in it. But I can make some drawings.'

'How long will that take?'

'One day, maybe two.'

'All right. You can stay here. We'll give you a room. Aisha will bring you food.'

The next two days passed quickly. Tim slept and worked in one of the rooms off the garden. He spent hour after hour on a careful drawing of each of the treasures, and he coloured each drawing. Aisha brought him meals, and at night he slept for a few hours.

The Professor sometimes visited his room, but Tim didn't see Maria again. 'What's happened to her?' he thought.

When he was almost finished, the Professor came into the room. He looked at Tim's drawings.

'They're good, very good,' he said. 'What will you do with them?'

'I'll show them to some people in the Cairo Museum and my own university, and I'll talk to some friends in the British Museum in London. And then I want to write an article about them.'

'But you won't forget your promise. You won't say where you saw these things.'

'Don't worry. I won't. Where's Maria? I haven't seen her. I wanted to talk to her about getting a new camera.'

'You can't. She isn't here. She's staying with her aunt at Abukir.'

'Oh! But she didn't say goodbye to me.'

'She didn't have time.'

Tim continued with his work. He was pleased with his drawings. He knew his discovery was an important one. He smiled as he imagined his return to London.

'I'll give talks. I'll write about it. I'll appear on television programmes. I'll be able to make a special study of the last of the pharaohs. Finally, I'll come back to Alexandria to find Cleopatra's tomb. I'm sure I can find it.'

He worked into the evening to finish the last drawing.

'Eat. Your food is ready.' Aisha put some food down on the table and left the room.

'Mmm! Thanks.' Tim put the drawings away carefully. He was very hungry. The food smelt very good. But as he picked up the plate, he saw a piece of paper.

It was hidden under the plate. He picked it up and read it.

The note was in English:

You are in terrible danger. Meet me in Saad Zaghlul Square at ten o'clock tonight.

'How can I be in danger?' Tim thought. 'Who wrote this? Is it a joke? Did Maria write it?'

Tim began to eat, but he wasn't hungry. He was worried. He looked at his watch. It was nine o'clock.

'How can I get to Saad Zaghlul Square from here?' he said to himself. 'I don't even know where I am.' He felt tired, and ready for bed. 'I have to leave early tomorrow,' he thought. He lay down, but he couldn't forget the message. 'What danger? Perhaps there really *is* some danger.'

There was pale moonlight in the garden. 'Ah! The moon is coming out,' Tim thought. 'I can keep it on my right and walk as far as the sea. Then I'll turn and walk to the square.'

He sat up. 'Right, I'm going to meet this mysterious person,' he decided. 'I'll close my door and turn the lights off. Felix and his father will think I'm asleep.'

He crossed the garden quietly, and opened the old wooden door. There were a lot of people in the street. Tim shut the door behind him, and looked for the moon.

Chapter 6   Flowers of Death

As Tim walked along the streets with the moonlight over his right shoulder, he looked around him. All along the way, shopkeepers were closing their shops for the night. Men were drinking a glass of tea or coffee in the cafés before they went home. The moonlight became brighter, and in the little squares off the narrow streets, sellers of fruit and cakes got ready for the evening's business. The crowd was thicker as Tim got nearer the sea.

'Oh, no!' Tim thought suddenly. 'How am I going to find my way back to the house? I don't even have the address.

He tried to turn back, but the crowd carried him with it. Soon he saw that the crowd was taking him into Saad Zaghlul Square. When they got to the square, people began to move away. Tim walked into the flower garden in the centre of the square.

'OK. Here I am in Saad Zaghlul Square, but where exactly am I going to meet Mr Mysterious? And how am I going to find my way back to the house?'

He looked at his watch. It was a quarter to ten. 'I'll walk round and round the square until something happens,' he decided.

He began walking. It took a long time to walk right round the square. Nobody even looked at Tim. He got back to the point where he started at. His watch showed five past ten. He went round the square again. 'I hope this isn't a joke. I really do.'

As he went round for the third time, he heard a quiet voice: 'Mr Saunders!'

Tim looked round. There was nobody in that part of the square.

'Mr Saunders!'

He looked up at a window high above him in a building on the east side of the square. 'Who is it?'

'Wait for me there. I am coming down.'

A few minutes later, a door opened and a woman hurried out. She ran over to Tim.

'Maria! What are you doing here? What's this about?'

'Come with me. I will explain everything later. We can't stay here. Nobody must see us.'

They went quickly through the streets.

'Where are we going?' Tim asked.

'Ssh! Hurry! We're nearly there. This is the place. Come in here.'

They were at a large, open gate.

'But it's a garden!'

'Yes. Very few people come here. We can talk.'

They walked through the garden. There was a beautiful smell of flowers. Trees reached out in the moonlight and touched their faces.

'Did you write me that note?'

'Yes, I did.'

'Why aren't you at Abukir?'

'Abukir?'

'Haven't you been with your aunt at Abukir?'

'So that's what my father told you!' Maria sounded angry. 'It isn't true! I haven't been anywhere. My father locked me in my room the first day that you came.'

'What? But why?'

'He didn't want me to talk to you.'

'Why not? And why did you write that I'm in terrible danger?'

Maria didn't reply immediately. She seemed to be thinking. She lifted her head and smelt the air. Then she turned to Tim.

'Come this way,' she said. 'I've got something to show you.'

By now Tim could also smell the sweet perfume that Maria seemed to be following. She took him along narrow paths, past dry pools full of dead leaves, and tall trees. The smell of perfume in the night air became stronger.

'What is it?' Tim wanted to know.

'Look!'

They were in an open area. In its centre there was a tree. It was covered with large white flowers. The lovely white flowers shone in the moonlight, and the air was full of their perfume.

'*Datura!*' Tim said softly.

'Yes. *Datura*. You know it?'

'Why are you showing me this?'

'This plant is beautiful – maybe more beautiful than any other plant. The shape of the flowers and the sweetness of their perfume are beautiful. But *datura* means 'death'. The plant is poisonous. It is beautiful, but there is also terrible danger – sometimes death.'

'What are you trying to tell me?'

'The treasure at my father's house is like this plant. It is beautiful, but it hides death.'

'What are you talking about?'

Maria picked one of the poisonous flowers and looked at it. 'There is a curse on the treasure. If anyone tries to take it, they will surely die!'

Chapter 7   The Curse of the Cobra

Maria looked at the tree while she touched the flower softly against her mouth.

'Stop that. It's poisonous.'

Tim took the flower from Maria. She looked up at him, surprised. In the pale moonlight, her face shone like the *datura* flowers.

'Maria, you're beautiful.'

She looked at him for a long time, then walked away. 'Didn't you hear what I said? About the curse on the treasure – that you will die if you take it?'

'I'm sorry,' Tim said softly. 'Tell me about the curse. Let's sit there.' He pointed to an old stone seat on the other side of the open area.

'No. Not there. Not anywhere near that plant.'

They left the open area. They found a seat by an old wall covered with climbing plants.

'Tell me,' said Tim.

Maria was silent for a time, and then began: 'You know about the curse of the tomb of Tutankhamen. And what happened to the archaeologists who discovered the tomb. They took the treasures, and they all died young. For no reason, it seemed. But there was a reason – the curse – the curse killed them– '

'Not so fast!' said Tim, laughing. 'Yes, I know the story.'

'Well, there's a curse on our treasure, too.'

'Why do you think that?'

'It's the curse of the cobra.'

'The cobra?'

'Yes. This cobra.'

Maria held up her wrist. The cobra lifted up its gold head; its red eyes shone in the moonlight. Tim looked at it for a long time.

Maria continued: 'When the pharaoh, the owner of the treasure, was near death, he put a white cobra in his tomb. Cobras live for hundreds of years. The pharaoh wanted it to protect him and his tomb from robbers. He ordered the cobra to look after his body and the treasures for ever. Then he put a curse, a terrible curse, on anyone who tried to take the treasure away. He died soon after that, and his body was prepared for the life after death.

'Food, drink, furniture, games, many things were put into the pharaoh's tomb. All the things were for the pharaoh to use in his next life. And, of course, the pharaoh's treasure was put in his tomb – but not all of it.

'A thief stole some of the treasure. He hid it in the roof of his house–'

'You mean,' Tim said, 'that there's a lot more treasure in the tomb?'

'Listen to me! The pharaoh was put in the tomb, and the door was closed. The thief was happy with the treasure for a few days, but then he began to have terrible dreams. He always dreamed the same dream – that a white cobra attacked him. He couldn't sleep or eat. He grew thin and ill. He knew then that he was under the curse of the cobra. He must return the treasure to the dead pharaoh, or die. One night, he took the treasure back to the tomb. He put it on the sand in front of the door of the tomb.'

'What happened then?'

'The pharaoh's treasurer found the thief the next morning. He was in front of the tomb and he was dead. He died of a snake bite.'

Tim laughed. Maria looked at him angrily.

'You don't believe me? It's true! You must believe me! Our family must keep the treasure now! We must keep it for the pharaoh! One day the pharaoh will come back from the afterlife and ask for it! Believe me!' she shouted. 'People have tried to take the treasure away from our family. And they have all died! They died from the curse!'

Tim took Maria's hand.

'Maria, listen to me. Curses like that don't really exist. The cobra doesn't exist, either. It's an interesting story, but I don't believe in these things. You'll see. I'll be OK.'

'You won't! You won't! I know you won't!' Maria began to cry. 'You must believe me! You must go away. You mustn't do anything with my father's things. Please, please leave them!'

'I can't,' Tim said. 'They're too important to me.'

She spoke quickly: 'Please leave Alexandria now – this minute. There is only death for you here. Go now before it is too late.'

She stood up and disappeared into the darkness of the garden. Tim sat for a minute, thinking.

'Maria!'

He searched the garden for a long time, but he couldn't find her. When he reached the gate of the garden, an old woman came towards him. She had a suitcase – Tim's suitcase – in her hands. It was Aisha.

'Maria told me to come,' she said. 'Here is your bag. I have put all your things in it. Maria told me to take you to the station.'

'Wait! Did you put my drawings in my bag?'

'No, I didn't.'

'I'm not going to leave Alexandria without them. Take me back to the house. I must have those drawings.'

27

But the old woman turned and walked away.

'Aisha! Stop!' Tim shouted.

But Aisha didn't seem to hear him. He waited for a second, and then began to follow her back to the house.

Chapter 8   Tim is Famous

'And now here is my last drawing . . .'

Tim showed a large drawing of Cleopatra's wonderful head-dress to the crowd in the big room. There was silence at first, then everyone began to talk excitedly. Tim smiled happily. A number of reporters in the front took notes and photographs. The Treasure of Cleopatra's Tomb was a very good story.

Tim finished his talk. 'Does anyone have any questions?' He looked around the room?

One of the reporters stood up. 'What do we really know about Cleopatra?'

'She was a strange and beautiful woman. The discovery of her tomb will give us more information about her life.'

'I read that she killed prisoners in the prison at Alexandria. Is that true?'

'The information comes from Roman writers. She wanted to discover the easiest way to die. So she gave the prisoners different poisons. We know she gave them snake poison. She then watched them die. She wanted to see which poisons gave the least painful death.'

'And she chose snake poison for herself?'

'It seems so. Yes,' Tim said.

'Was her death easy?'

Tim answered, 'I don't know the answer to that question. Perhaps I'll be able to tell you after I discover her tomb. It's possible that there's still poison in her body.'

Tim left the room. A crowd of reporters followed him and shouted more questions. Tim turned round and faced them.

'I'll meet you all again at the end of the week. The information about my discoveries will appear in an article in tomorrow's *London News*. In the article you will be able to see my drawings and read my notes. You will also be able to read the story of how I found the treasure.'

Tim went into his study. He was glad to shut the door behind him. He didn't like being famous. He missed the quiet of the Egyptian desert. Even in the excitement of his discovery, something was missing.

'I'll go back to Alexandria soon,' he said to himself. 'I'll see Maria. I'll explain why I had to get my drawings back . . .'

He went to his desk. There were a lot of letters. Most of them were from other archaeologists, asking questions about his discovery. There was one letter in a brown envelope with an Egyptian stamp. Tim opened it. It was from the Egyptian government. He read it quickly:

. . . Do you know that it is against the law in this country for anyone to own treasure from the tombs of the Pharaohs? All treasure belongs to the government. . . . You must tell us immediately where . . . crime . . . prison . . .

Tim sat down. He read the letter again, carefully.

'I don't believe it! They think I've got the treasure! They think I've stolen it!' Tim thought for a minute. 'Well, I haven't got the treasure. I've only got my drawings. I'll tell them that!'

Then he suddenly felt cold.

'I can tell them that,' he thought, 'but will they believe me? How can I prove that I haven't got the treasure?'

Chapter 9   The Arrest

Tim got off the train in Alexandria. It was early morning. He got into a taxi. 'Take me to the old town,' he said to the driver.

The smells of the market came in through the open window of the taxi – the smell of cooking oil, of fresh bread, of chickens, of oranges and other fruit.

'What am I going to say to Maria's father? Will I be able to see Maria again? Will she be angry with me for getting my drawings?'

The taxi left the wide streets of the modern town and drove into the narrower streets of the old city.

'Where are you going to?' asked the driver in Arabic.

'Straight on,' Tim said. The taxi went straight on. Tim didn't know this street. 'No. Not this way. Go back again.'

'Go where?'

'I'm not sure – yes, I am. Take me to Saad Zaghlul Square.'

They arrived at the square.

'I'll get out here.' Tim paid the driver and picked up his case. 'Thank you. Now I'll be able to find my way.'

He walked along by the sea and then turned down one of the little streets.

'I'm sure it was down here.' Tim followed the street. It wasn't the right one. He tried another street, with no luck. He tried a third, but it wasn't the right one. The sun was now quite high in the sky. Tim was hot and his case was heavy.

'Excuse me. Do you know anyone called Felix? He has a sister called Maria. They live near here.' Tim stopped and asked a number of people, but nobody knew them.

Suddenly, on the other side of a little square, he saw Aisha. She was in front of small fruit shop. She took some money out of her bag and bought some oranges. Tim pushed through the shoppers to reach her.

'Aisha! I'm trying to find Maria's house, but I can't. Will you show me the way?'

The woman looked at Tim. She seemed angry. She said something that he didn't hear. Then she turned away.

'Please don't go. I have to see Maria. What's the matter?'

'I don't know anyone called Maria. Go away.'

'But you work for her. You came to the garden with my case. I followed you back to the house to get my drawings . . .'

The woman looked at Tim strangely. 'I don't know you,' she said again. Then she turned and disappeared into the crowd.

'Wait! Wait!' Tim shouted. But it was too late.

'I know it was her,' thought Tim. 'I'm sure it was her. It was her. Why didn't she want to talk to me?'

Tim felt very tired. He went into a café and ordered tea. It *was* late in the afternoon now, and Tim was hot, tired and dirty.

'I've got to find them.' He began to search every street, but all the streets and all the wooden doors looked the same.

'Well, I'll have to begin again tomorrow,' Tim thought.

He found a hotel for the night. The next morning, he bought a street map of Alexandria. For two days, he looked at every house in every street in the old town. He looked very carefully, but he didn't find the house.

'I don't understand,' he said to himself at the end of the second day. 'The house isn't there. It's disappeared.'

Tim took a train back to Cairo. He went straight to the airport from the station, and bought a ticket back to London.

'Excuse me, sir.'

Tim looked round. There were two men behind him. 'Yes?'

'You are Mr Tim Saunders?'

'Yes.

'We are from the police. Please come with us.'

'Why? What do you want? Where are we going?' asked Tim.

'Come!' they replied.

Tim followed them quietly. The two policemen took Tim into an office. A man was sitting behind the desk, with a magazine in front of him. It was the *London News*. On the front, there was a full-page drawing of the cobra bracelet.

'My article. Why have you got that?'

'You've heard of tomb-robbing, haven't you?'

'Yes, yes, of course I have.'

'Tomb-robbing is a very serious crime, a *very* serious crime. A lot of treasure is still hidden in the sand, and sometimes the wrong people find it. They sell it, but this is against the law.'

'I know that.'

'Tomb robbers today have two main problems. First, they have to prove that their discoveries are real. If they can't prove that, they won't get a good price. Then they have to get information about their discoveries to the people who want to buy ancient treasures. The robbers want private buyers all over the world to know about the treasure. They want publicity. With publicity, the robbers will get the highest possible price.'

'I understand,' Tim said.

'The best-known team of tomb robbers works for an old man – a very clever old man. He calls himself the Professor, and he works with his son and daughter. The son's name is Felix and the daughter is called Maria.'

'What?' Tim shouted. 'It's not true! I don't believe it!'

'Sit down, please, Mr Saunders,' the policeman said. 'You, Mr Saunders, have helped these robbers. You have shown that their discoveries are real. Your article has given publicity to their treasure everywhere in the world. Nobody will ever see the treasures of the tomb of Cleopatra again. They will stay hidden from the world in a rich man's private jewellery box.'

Tim held onto the table to stop himself falling. He sat down quickly, and closed his eyes.

'Well,' said one of the policemen, 'what do you say to that?'

'Nothing,' Tim said quietly. He put his face in his hands and tried to hide his tears.

'We know you are a tomb robber. And we know why you have come back into this country.'

'Why?' Tim asked.

'You want your money, don't you?'

Chapter 10   Free at Last

Tim woke up. It was morning, and the sun was shining through the prison window.

'It's today. I'm going to be free, free after five years.' Tim jumped to his feet. 'Free!'

He hard the sound of running feet.

'Why are you shouting?' asked the guard.

'I'm going to be free!' Tim replied.

He followed the guard to the office.

'Here are the clothes and things that you came here with.'

Tim looked at the little pile. A book, a pen, a pencil, a chequebook, a little money. Then he picked up something that looked like a dirty piece of paper.

'What's this?' He looked at it carefully. 'Oh! It's the *datura* flower. The flower that she picked. Beautiful but poisonous.'

Tim put the dried flower into his pocket. The guard took him through the prison, and unlocked the heavy door. Tim walked a few steps into the open air.

'Now,' he thought, 'where shall I go first? What shall I do?'

'Tim!'

He looked round. A woman sat in an expensive white car on the other side of the street. She smiled and waved at him.

'Maria?. . . Maria! What are you doing here?'

He crossed the road.

'You are late. I have been here for half an hour!' She opened the passenger door. 'Get in! I will explain,' she said.

'Where did you get this car? Where are your father and brother? Why didn't you stop them doing this to me?'

Maria started the car. She drove away from the prison.

'Where are we going?'

'To Alexandria by the desert road.' They drove for some time in silence.

'I tried to stop my father and brother,' said Maria. 'I didn't want you to be hurt. But my brother told me not to be stupid, and my father locked me in my room.'

'It was lucky for your brother that he met me on the train.'

'It wasn't luck. We had a list of the archaeologists at that meeting in Cairo. My father chose you. Then we followed you from your hotel to the station. We learnt your seat number at the ticket office. Then we got to the seats opposite yours before you got on the train.'

Tim looked at her in surprise. 'You mean you planned everything, from the beginning?'

'Yes, it was all planned – even the changes to the appearance of our house. It wasn't my idea. I told you to leave, but you wanted the drawings. I'm sorry that I didn't destroy them.'

'Where's the treasure?'

'In America.'

'And where are the Professor and Felix?'

'They're dead.'

'What?' Tim asked in surprise. 'Both of them? Dead? What happened?'

'They were bitten by a snake – a cobra.'

Tim's face went white. 'The curse of the cobra!'

Maria shook her head. 'No. The curse doesn't exist.'

'What? But you told me about it.'

'It was just a story,' said Maria. 'That night in the garden, when

I warned you to leave, I couldn't tell you the true story. My father and brother were using you. They wanted publicity for the treasure. I didn't know what to say. Then I thought of the story, that there was a curse on the treasure. I knew about the curse of the tomb of Tutankhamen. I got the idea of the snake from the bracelet that I was wearing. I wanted to frighten you. I'm sorry it didn't work. I wanted to tell you about my father and brother, but I didn't want my father to get into trouble.'

Tim looked out at the desert. 'How were they bitten by the snake?'

Maria looked a little uncomfortable. 'They found a Ptolemaic tomb, near Alexandria. Probably Cleopatra's tomb. They decided to break into the tomb the next evening. They were near the tomb when they were bitten by a cobra. I found them the next morning. Next to them was a map showing the position of the tomb, and some notes. I – I have those notes and the map.'

'What? Do you mean it? You've got a map? A map showing the position of Cleopatra's tomb? And your father's notes? Then we can do it! We'll do it together, you and I!'

'Do what?' asked Maria, smiling.

'Discover the tomb, find its treasure, show it to the world, give it to the museum in Cairo!'

Maria laughed. 'You haven't changed.'

She sang softly to herself as they drove through the desert.

'Ssh!'

'What?'

'Didn't you hear anything?'

'Hear what?' Maria stopped singing.

Tim heard the sound again. He looked round – and his heart stopped. On the back seat of the car there was a snake – a very large, very old white snake. Its head was very close to him. Tim watched it, unable to move.

Then Maria saw it too, and screamed: 'The cobra!'

ACTIVITIES

Chapters 1–3

Before you read

1 The book is called *The Great Discovery*. Discuss these questions.

    a The story takes place in Egypt. What great discoveries have there been in Egypt?

    b Can you name three great discoveries in other parts of the world?

2 Find these words in your dictionary. They are all in the story. Do they describe people, animals or buildings?

    archaeologist   cobra   museum   pharaoh   snake   tomb

People	Animals	Buildings
....	....	....
....	....	....

3 What do the words in *italics* mean? Choose the right ending to each sentence.

    a *Ancient* means:

    very new   very old   very bad

    b You wear *bracelets* around your:

    head   legs   wrists

    c You keep *jewels* (*jewellery*) in:

    a fridge   a car   a box

After you read

4 How does Tim feel about these people? Give reasons.

    a Ahmed

    b Maria

    c Felix

5 Describe the bracelet. Why is Tim so interested in it?

Chapters 4–6

Before you read

6 Read these sentences. What do you think the words in *italics* mean?

   a The woman in white suddenly *appeared* in the room.

   b Have you read today's paper? There's an *article* about tourism in Egypt.

   c There's a *curse* on this ship. A passenger dies on every trip!

   d You smell nice! What *perfume* are you wearing?

   e No! Don't drink that! It's *poison*!

   f He's a *professor* at the university.

   g I know the *treasure* is hidden somewhere under the ground.

   h You *warned* me about the danger! Why didn't I listen to you?

   Now check the meanings of the new words in your dictionary. Were you right?

7 Chapter 5 is called 'A Mysterious Warning'. What do you think the warning is about? Why is Tim in danger?

After you read

8 Does Tim think that the treasure is real? Why (not)?

9 Work in pairs. Act out this conversation.

   Student A: You are Tim. Ask the Professor about the treasure. You want to know where it comes from. Is there more?

   Student B: You are the Professor. You don't want to tell Tim anything.

Chapters 7–10

Before you read

10 Discuss these questions.

   a Do you think Tim will make his great discovery?

   b How do you think the story will end?

11 Find these words in your dictionary:

   arrest   desert   publicity

Which word is connected with:

a the police?

b television?

c hot sun?

After you read

12 Why are these important to the story?

    a the article in the *London News*

    b the letter to Tim from the Egyptian government

    c the map that Maria found by the bodies of Felix and the Professor

13 Do you think the Professor and Felix were killed by the curse? Give your reasons.

Writing

14 Imagine that you are Tim. Write about the day when you met Felix, Maria and the Professor.

15 Maria wrote a note warning Tim to leave Alexandria. Write the note.

16 Write Tim's article about the jewellery for the *London News*.

17 Imagine that you work for an English-language newspaper in Egypt. What happened to Tim and Maria as they drove through the desert to Alexandria? Write an article.

Answers for the Activities in this book are published in our free resource packs for teachers, the Penguin Readers Factsheets, or available on a separate sheet. Please write to your local Pearson Education office or to: Marketing Department, Penguin Longman Publishing, 5 Bentinck Street, London W1M 5RN.